The Marquise De Ganges

by

Alexandre Dumas, Pere

The Marquise De Ganges
by Alexandre Dumas, Pere

ISBN: 978-93-59953-35-9

Published by

DOUBLE 9 BOOKS

2/13-B, Ansari Road
Daryaganj, New Delhi – 110002
info@double9books.com
www.double9books.com
Tel. 011-40042856

This book is under public domain

ABOUT THE AUTHOR

Alexandre Dumas, père, changed into a prolific and influential French author of the nineteenth century, born on July 24, 1802, in Villers-Cotterêts, France. Dumas is celebrated for his historic novels and journey tales, which have left an indelible mark on world literature. His masterpieces, which includes "The Three Musketeers" and "The Count of Monte Cristo," are revered for his or her swashbuckling pleasure, elaborate plots, and noteworthy characters. Dumas's works often explore issues of honor, loyalty, and justice against wealthy historic backdrops, showcasing his keen understanding of human nature and societal intricacies. His writing style is characterized with the aid of a dynamic narrative, humor, and a deep information of the complexities of human relationships. A man of blended African and European heritage, Dumas faced challenges associated with racial prejudice in his lifetime, however his literary achievements transcended such boundaries. His adventurous spirit and unbridled creativeness retain to captivate readers worldwide, making him one of the maximum extensively examine and loved authors in history. Alexandre Dumas, père, remains a literary icon, and his timeless memories continue to encourage and entertain generations of readers, making sure his enduring legacy in the global of literature.

CONTENTS

THE MARQUISE DE GANGES—1657

Toward the close of the year 1657, a very plain carriage, with no arms painted on it, stopped, about eight o'clock one evening, before the door of a house in the rue Hautefeuille, at which two other coaches were already standing. A lackey at once got down to open the carriage door; but a sweet, though rather tremulous voice stopped him, saying, "Wait, while I see whether this is the place."

Then a head, muffled so closely in a black satin mantle that no feature could be distinguished, was thrust from one of the carriage windows, and looking around, seemed to seek for some decisive sign on the house front. The unknown lady appeared to be satisfied by her inspection, for she turned back to her companion.

"It is here," said she. "There is the sign."

As a result of this certainty, the carriage door was opened, the two women alighted, and after having once more raised their eyes to a strip of wood, some six or eight feet long by two broad, which was nailed above the windows of the second storey, and bore the inscription, "Madame Voison, midwife," stole quickly into a passage, the door of which was unfastened, and in which there was just so much light as enabled persons passing in or out to find their way along the narrow winding stair that led from the ground floor to the fifth story.

The two strangers, one of whom appeared to be of far higher rank than the other, did not stop, as might have been expected, at the door corresponding with the inscription that had guided them, but, on the contrary, went on to the next floor.

Here, upon the landing, was a kind of dwarf, oddly dressed after the fashion of sixteenth-century Venetian buffoons, who, when he saw the two women coming, stretched out a wand, as though to prevent them from going farther, and asked what they wanted.

"To consult the spirit," replied the woman of the sweet and tremulous voice.

"Come in and wait," returned the dwarf, lifting a panel of tapestry and ushering the two women into a waiting-room.

The women obeyed, and remained for about half an hour, seeing and hearing nothing. At last a door, concealed by the tapestry, was suddenly opened; a voice uttered the word "Enter," and the two women were introduced into a second room, hung with black, and lighted solely by a three-branched lamp that hung from the ceiling. The door closed behind them, and the clients found themselves face to face with the sibyl.

She was a woman of about twenty-five or twenty-six, who, unlike other women, evidently desired to appear older than she was. She was dressed in black; her hair hung in plaits; her neck, arms, and feet were bare; the belt at her waist was clasped by a large garnet which threw out sombre fires. In her hand she held a wand, and she was raised on a sort of platform which stood for the tripod of the ancients, and from which came acrid and penetrating fumes; she was, moreover, fairly handsome, although her features were common, the eyes only excepted, and these, by some trick of the toilet, no doubt, looked inordinately large, and, like the garnet in her belt, emitted strange lights.

When the two visitors came in, they found the soothsayer leaning her forehead on her hand, as though absorbed in thought. Fearing to rouse her from her ecstasy, they waited in silence until it should please her to change her position. At the end of ten minutes she raised her head, and seemed only now to become aware that two persons were standing before her.

"What is wanted of me again?" she asked, "and shall I have rest only in the grave?"

"Forgive me, madame," said the sweet-voiced unknown, "but I am wishing to know——"

"Silence!" said the sibyl, in a solemn voice. "I will not know your affairs. It is to the spirit that you must address yourself; he is a jealous spirit, who forbids his secrets to be shared; I can but pray to him for you, and obey his will."

At these words, she left her tripod, passed into an adjoining room, and soon returned, looking even paler and more anxious than before, and carrying in one hand a burning chafing dish, in the other a red paper. The three flames of the lamp grew fainter at the same moment, and the room was left lighted up only by the chafing dish; every object now assumed a fantastic air that did not fail to disquiet the two visitors, but it was too late to draw back.

The soothsayer placed the chafing dish in the middle of the room, presented the paper to the young woman who had spoken, and said to her—

"Write down what you wish to know."

The woman took the paper with a steadier hand than might have been expected, seated herself at a table, and wrote:—

"Am I young? Am I beautiful? Am I maid, wife, or widow? This is for the past.

"Shall I marry, or marry again? Shall I live long, or shall I die young? This is for the future."

Then, stretching out her hand to the soothsayer, she asked—

"What am I to do now with this?"

"Roll that letter around this ball," answered the other, handing to the unknown a little ball of virgin wax. "Both ball and letter will be consumed in the flame before your eyes; the spirit knows your secrets already. In three days you will have the answer."

The unknown did as the sibyl bade her; then the latter took from her hands the ball and the paper in which it was wrapped, and went and threw both into the chafing pan.

"And now all is done as it should be," said the soothsayer. "Comus!"

The dwarf came in.

"See the lady to her coach."

The stranger left a purse upon the table, and followed Comus. He conducted her and her companion, who was only a confidential maid, down a back staircase, used as an exit, and leading into a different street from that by which the two women had come in; but the coachman, who had been told beforehand of this circumstance, was awaiting them at the door, and they had only to step into their carriage, which bore them rapidly away in the direction of the rue Dauphine.

Three days later, according to the promise given her, the fair unknown, when she awakened, found on the table beside her a letter in an unfamiliar handwriting; it was addressed "To the beautiful Provencale," and contained these words—

"You are young; you are beautiful; you are a widow. This is for the present.

"You will marry again; you will die young, and by a violent death. This is for the future.

The answer was written upon a paper like that upon which the questions had been set down.

The marquise turned pale and uttered a faint cry of terror; the answer was so perfectly correct in regard to the past as to call up a fear that it might be equally accurate in regard to the future.

The truth is that the unknown lady wrapped in a mantle whom we have escorted into the modern sibyl's cavern was no other than the beautiful Marie de Rossan, who before her marriage had borne the name of Mademoiselle de Chateaublanc, from that of an estate belonging to her maternal grandfather, M. Joannis de Nocheres, who owned a fortune of five to six hundred thousand livres. At the age of thirteen—that is to say, in 1649—she had married the Marquis de Castellane, a gentleman of very high birth, who claimed to be descended from John of Castille, the son of Pedro the Cruel, and from Juana de Castro, his mistress. Proud of his young wife's beauty, the Marquis de Castellane, who was an officer of the king's galleys, had hastened to present her at court. Louis XIV, who at the time of her presentation was barely twenty years old, was struck by her enchanting face, and to the great despair of the famous beauties of the day danced with her three times in one evening. Finally, as a crowning touch to her reputation, the famous Christina of Sweden, who was then at the French court, said of her that she had never, in any of the kingdoms through which she had passed, seen anything equal to "the beautiful Provencale." This praise had been so well received, that the name of "the beautiful Provencale" had clung to Madame de Castellane, and she was everywhere known by it.

This favour of Louis XIV and this summing up of Christina's had been enough to bring the Marquise de Castellane instantly into fashion; and Mignard, who had just received a patent of nobility and been made painter to the king, put the seal to her celebrity by asking leave to paint her portrait. That portrait still exists, and gives a perfect notion of the beauty which it represents; but as the portrait is far from our readers' eyes, we will content ourselves by repeating, in its own original words, the one given in 1667 by the author of a pamphlet published at Rouen under the following title: True and Principal Circumstances of the Deplorable Death of Madame the Marquise de Ganges:

[Note: It is from this pamphlet, and from the Account of the Death of Madame the Marquise de Ganges, formerly Marquise de Castellane, that we have borrowed the principal circumstances of this tragic story. To these documents we must add—that we may not be constantly referring our readers to original sources — the Celebrated Trials by Guyot de Pitaval, the Life of Marie de Rossan, and the Lettres galantes of Madame Desnoyers.]

"Her complexion, which was of a dazzling whiteness, was illumined by not too brilliant a red, and art itself could not have arranged more skilfully the gradations by which this red joined and merged into the whiteness of the complexion. The brilliance of her face was heightened by the decided blackness of her hair, growing, as though drawn by a painter of the finest taste, around a well proportioned brow; her large, well opened eyes were of the same hue as her hair, and shone with a soft and piercing flame that rendered it impossible to gaze upon her steadily; the smallness, the shape, the turn of her mouth, and, the beauty of her teeth were incomparable; the position and the regular proportion of her nose added to her beauty such an air of dignity, as inspired a respect for her equal to the love that might be inspired by her beauty; the rounded contour of her face, produced by a becoming plumpness, exhibited all the vigour and freshness of health; to complete her charms, her glances, the movements of her lips and of her head, appeared to be guided by the graces; her shape corresponded to the beauty of her face; lastly, her arms, her hands, her bearing, and her gait were such that nothing further could be wished to complete the agreeable presentment of a beautiful woman."

[Note: All her contemporaries, indeed, are in agreement as to her marvellous beauty; here is a second portrait of the marquise, delineated in a style and manner still more characteristic of that period: —

"You will remember that she had a complexion smoother and finer than a mirror, that her whiteness was so well commingled with the lively blood as to produce an exact admixture never beheld elsewhere, and imparting to her countenance the tenderest animation; her eyes and hair were blacker than jet; her eyes, I say, of which the gaze could scarce, from their excess of lustre, be supported, which have been celebrated as a miracle of tenderness and sprightliness, which have given rise, a thousand times, to the finest compliments of the day, and have been the torment of many a rash man, must excuse me, if I do not pause longer to praise them, in a letter; her mouth was the feature of her face which compelled the most critical to avow that they had seen none of equal perfection, and that, by its shape, its smallness, and its brilliance, it might furnish a pattern for all those others whose sweetness and charms had been so highly vaunted; her nose conformed to the fair proportion of all her features; it was, that is to say, the finest in the world; the whole shape of her face was perfectly round, and of so charming a fullness that such an assemblage of beauties was never before seen together. The expression of this head was one of unparalleled sweetness and of a majesty which she softened rather by disposition than by study; her figure was opulent, her speech agreeable, her step noble, her demeanour easy, her temper sociable, her wit devoid of malice, and founded upon great goodness of heart."]

It is easy to understand that a woman thus endowed could not, in a court where gallantry was more pursued than in any other spot in the world, escape the calumnies of rivals; such calumnies, however, never produced any result, so correctly, even in the absence of her husband, did the marquise contrive to conduct herself; her cold and serious conversation, rather concise than lively, rather solid than brilliant, contrasted, indeed, with the light turn, the capricious and fanciful expressions employed by the wits of that time; the consequence was that those who had failed to succeed with her, tried to spread a report that the marquise was merely a beautiful idol, virtuous with the virtue of a statue. But though such things might be said and repeated in the absence of the marquise, from the moment that she appeared in a drawing-room, from the moment that her beautiful eyes and sweet smile added their indefinable expression to those brief, hurried, and sensible words that fell from her lips, the most prejudiced came back to her and were forced to own that God had never before created anything that so nearly touched perfection.

She was thus in the enjoyment of a triumph that backbiters failed to shake, and that scandal vainly sought to tarnish, when news came of the wreck of the French galleys in Sicilian waters, and of the death of the Marquis de Castellane, who was in command. The marquise on this occasion, as usual, displayed the greatest piety and propriety: although she had no very violent passion for her husband, with whom she had spent scarcely one of the seven years during which their marriage had lasted, on receipt of the news she went at once into retreat, going to live with Madame d'Ampus, her mother-in-law, and ceasing not only to receive visitors but also to go out.

Six months after the death of her husband, the marquise received letters from her grandfather, M. Joannis de Nocheres, begging her to come and finish her time of mourning at Avignon. Having been fatherless almost from childhood, Mademoiselle de Chateaublanc had been brought up by this good old man, whom she loved dearly; she hastened accordingly to accede to his invitation, and prepared everything for her departure.

This was at the moment when la Voisin, still a young woman, and far from having the reputation which she subsequently acquired, was yet beginning to be talked of. Several friends of the Marquise de Castellane had been to consult her, and had received strange predictions from her, some of which, either through the art of her who framed them, or through some odd concurrence of circumstances, had come true. The marquise could not resist the curiosity with which various tales that she had heard of this woman's powers had inspired her, and some days before setting out for Avignon she made the visit which we have narrated. What answer she received to her questions we have seen.

The marquise was not superstitious, yet this fatal prophecy impressed itself upon her mind and left behind a deep trace, which neither the pleasure of revisiting her native place, nor the affection of her grandfather, nor the fresh admiration which she did not fail to receive, could succeed in removing; indeed, this fresh admiration was a weariness to the marquise, and before long she begged leave of her grandfather to retire into a convent and to spend there the last three months of her mourning.

It was in that place, and it was with the warmth of these poor cloistered maidens, that she heard a man spoken of for the first time, whose reputation for beauty, as a man, was equal to her own, as a woman. This favourite of nature was the sieur de Lenide, Marquis de Ganges, Baron of Languedoc, and governor of Saint-Andre, in the diocese of Uzes. The marquise heard of him so often, and it was so frequently declared to her that nature seemed to have formed them for each other, that she began to allow admission to a very strong desire of seeing him. Doubtless, the sieur de Lenide, stimulated by similar suggestions, had conceived a great wish to meet the marquise; for, having got M. de Nocheres who no doubt regretted her prolonged retreat—to entrust him with a commission for his granddaughter, he came to the convent parlour and asked for the fair recluse. She, although she had never seen him, recognised him at the first glance; for having never seen so handsome a cavalier as he who now presented himself before her, she thought this could be no other than the Marquis de Ganges, of whom people had so often spoken to her.

That which was to happen, happened: the Marquise de Castellane and the Marquis de Ganges could not look upon each other without loving. Both were young, the marquis was noble and in a good position, the marquise was rich; everything in the match, therefore, seemed suitable: and indeed it was deferred only for the space of time necessary to complete the year of mourning, and the marriage was celebrated towards the beginning of the year 1558. The marquis was twenty years of age, and the marquise twenty-two.

The beginnings of this union were perfectly happy; the marquis was in love for the first time, and the marquise did not remember ever to have been in love. A son and a daughter came to complete their happiness. The marquise had entirely forgotten the fatal prediction, or, if she occasionally thought of it now, it was to wonder that she could ever have believed in it. Such happiness is not of this world, and when by chance it lingers here a while, it seems sent rather by the anger than by the goodness of God. Better, indeed, would it be for him who possesses and who loses it, never to have known it.

The Marquis de Ganges was the first to weary of this happy life. Little by little he began to miss the pleasures of a young man; he began to draw away from the marquise and to draw nearer to his former friends. On her part, the marquise, who for the sake of wedded intimacy had sacrificed her habits of social life, threw herself into society, where new triumphs awaited her. These triumphs aroused the jealousy of the marquis; but he was too much a man of his century to invite ridicule by any manifestation; he shut his jealousy into his soul, and it emerged in a different form on every different occasion. To words of love, so sweet that they seemed the speech of angels, succeeded those bitter and biting utterances that foretell approaching division. Before long, the marquis and the marquise only saw each other at hours when they could not avoid meeting; then, on the pretext of necessary journeys, and presently without any pretext at all, the marquis would go away for three-quarters of a year, and once more the marquise found herself widowed. Whatever contemporary account one may consult, one finds them all agreeing to declare that she was always the same—that is to say, full of patience, calmness, and becoming behaviour—and it is rare to find such a unanimity of opinion about a young and beautiful woman.

About this time the marquis, finding it unendurable to be alone with his wife during the short spaces of time which he spent at home, invited his two brothers, the chevalier and the abbe de Ganges, to come and live with him. He had a third brother, who, as the second son, bore the title of comte, and who was colonel of the Languedoc regiment, but as this gentleman played no part in this story we shall not concern ourselves with him.

The abbe de Ganges, who bore that title without belonging to the Church, had assumed it in order to enjoy its privileges: he was a kind of wit, writing madrigals and 'bouts-rimes' [Bouts-rimes are verses written to a given set of rhymes.] on occasion, a handsome man enough, though in moments of impatience his eyes would take a strangely cruel expression; as dissolute and shameless to boot, as though he had really belonged to the clergy of the period.

The chevalier de Ganges, who shared in some measure the beauty so profusely showered upon the family, was one of those feeble men who enjoy their own nullity, and grow on to old age inapt alike for good and evil, unless some nature of a stronger stamp lays hold on them and drags them like faint and pallid satellites in its wake. This was what befell the chevalier in respect of his brother: submitted to an influence of which he himself was not aware, and against which, had he but suspected it, he would have rebelled with the obstinacy of a child, he was a machine obedient to the will of another mind and to the passions of another heart, a machine which was all the more terrible in that no movement of instinct or of reason could, in his case, arrest the impulse given.

Moreover, this influence which the abbe had acquired over the chevalier extended, in some degree also, to the marquis. Having as a younger son no fortune, having no revenue, for though he wore a Churchman's robes he did not fulfil a Churchman's functions, he had succeeded in persuading the marquis, who was rich, not only in the enjoyment of his own fortune, but also in that of his wife, which was likely to be nearly doubled at the death of M. de Nocheres, that some zealous man was needed who would devote himself to the ordering of his house and the management of his property; and had offered himself for the post. The marquis had very gladly accepted, being, as we have said, tired by this time of his solitary home life; and the abbe had brought with him the chevalier, who followed him like his shadow, and who was no more regarded than if he had really possessed no body.

The marquise often confessed afterwards that when she first saw these two men, although their outward aspect was perfectly agreeable, she felt herself seized by a painful impression, and that the fortune-teller's prediction of a violent death, which she had so long forgotten, gashed out like lightning before her eyes. The effect on the two brothers was not of the same kind: the beauty of the marquise struck them both, although in different ways. The chevalier was in ecstasies of admiration, as though before a beautiful statue, but the impression that she made upon him was that which would have been made by marble, and if the chevalier had been left to himself the consequences of this admiration would have been no less harmless. Moreover, the chevalier did not attempt either to exaggerate or to conceal this impression, and allowed his sister-in-law to see in what manner she struck him. The abbe, on the contrary, was seized at first sight with a deep and violent desire to possess this woman—the most beautiful whom he had ever met; but being as perfectly capable of mastering his sensations as the chevalier was incapable, he merely allowed such words of compliment to escape him as weigh neither with him who utters nor her who hears them; and yet, before the close of this first interview, the abbe had decided in his irrevocable will that this woman should be his.

As for the marquise, although the impression produced by her two brothers-in-law could never be entirely effaced, the wit of the abbe, to which he gave, with amazing facility, whatever turn he chose, and the complete nullity of the chevalier brought her to certain feelings of less repulsion towards them: for indeed the marquise had one of those souls which never suspect evil, as long as it will take the trouble to assume any veil at all of seeming, and which only recognise it with regret when it resumes its true shape.

Meanwhile the arrival of these two new inmates soon spread a little more life and gaiety through the house. Furthermore; greatly to the astonishment of the marquise, her husband, who had so long been indifferent to her beauty, seemed to remark afresh that she was too charming to be despised; his words accordingly began little by little to express an affection that had long since gradually disappeared from them. The marquise had never ceased to love him; she had suffered the loss of his love with resignation, she hailed its return with joy, and three months elapsed that resembled those which had long ceased to be more to the poor wife than a distant and half-worn-out memory.

Thus she had, with the supreme facility of youth, always ready to be happy, taken up her gladness again, without even asking what genius had brought back to her the treasure which she had thought lost, when she received an invitation from a lady of the neighbourhood to spend some days in her country house. Her husband and her two brothers-in-law, invited with her, were of the party, and accompanied her. A great hunting party had been arranged beforehand, and almost immediately upon arriving everyone began to prepare for taking part in it.

The abbe, whose talents had made him indispensable in every company, declared that for that day he was the marquise's cavalier, a title which his sister-in-law, with her usual amiability, confirmed. Each of the huntsmen, following this example, made choice of a lady to whom to dedicate his attentions throughout the day; then, this chivalrous arrangement being completed, all present directed their course towards the place of meeting.

That happened which almost always happens the dogs hunted on their own account. Two or three sportsmen only followed the dogs; the rest got lost. The abbe, in his character of esquire to the marquise, had not left her for a moment, and had managed so cleverly that he was alone with her—an opportunity which he had been seeking for a month previously with no less care—than the marquise had been using to avoid it. No sooner, therefore, did the marquise believe herself aware that the abbe had intentionally turned aside from the hunt than she attempted to gallop her horse in the opposite direction from that which she had been following; but the abbe stopped her. The marquise neither could nor would enter upon a struggle; she resigned herself, therefore, to hearing what the abbe had to say to her, and her face assumed that air of haughty disdain which women so well know how to put on when they wish a man to understand that he has nothing to hope from them. There was an instant's silence; the abbe was the first to break it.

"Madame," said he, "I ask your pardon for having used this means to speak to you alone; but since, in spite of my rank of brother-in-law, you did not seem inclined to grant me that favour if I had asked it, I thought it would be better for me, to deprive you of the power to refuse it me."

"If you have hesitated to ask me so simple a thing, monsieur," replied the marquise, "and if you have taken such precautions to compel me to listen to you, it must, no doubt, be because you knew beforehand that the words you had to say to me were such as I could not hear. Have the goodness, therefore, to reflect, before you open this conversation, that here as elsewhere I reserve the right—and I warn you of it—to interrupt what you may say at the moment when it may cease to seem to me befitting."

"As to that, madame," said the abbe, "I think I can answer for it that whatever it may please me to say to you, you will hear to the end; but indeed the matters are so simple that there is no need to make you uneasy beforehand: I wished to ask you, madame, whether you have perceived a change in the conduct of your husband towards you."

"Yes, monsieur," replied the marquise, "and no single day has passed in which I have not thanked Heaven for this happiness."

"And you have been wrong, madame," returned the abbe, with one of those smiles that were peculiar to himself; "Heaven has nothing to do with it. Thank Heaven for having made you the most beautiful and charming of women, and that will be enough thanksgiving without despoiling me of such as belong to my share."

"I do not understand you, monsieur," said the marquise in an icy tone.

"Well, I will make myself comprehensible, my dear sister-in-law. I am the worker of the miracle for which you are thanking Heaven; to me therefore belongs your gratitude. Heaven is rich enough not to rob the poor."

"You are right, monsieur: if it is really to you that I owe this return, the cause of which I did not know, I will thank you in the first place; and then afterwards I will thank Heaven for having inspired you with this good thought."

"Yes," answered the abbe, "but Heaven, which has inspired me with a good thought, may equally well inspire me with a bad one, if the good thought does not bring me what I expect from it."

"What do you mean, monsieur?"

"That there has never been more than one will in the family, and that will is mine; that the minds of my two brothers turn according to the fancy of that will like weathercocks before the wind, and that he who has blown hot can blow cold."

"I am still waiting for you to explain yourself, monsieur."

"Well, then, my dear sister-in-law, since you are pleased not to understand me, I will explain myself more clearly. My brother turned from you through jealousy; I wished to give you an idea of my power over him, and from extreme indifference I have brought him back, by showing him that he suspected you wrongly, to the ardours of the warmest love. Well, I need only tell him that I was mistaken, and fix his wandering suspicions upon any man whatever, and I shall take him away from you, even as I have brought him back. I need give you no proof of what I say; you know perfectly well that I am speaking the truth."

"And what object had you, in acting this part?"

"To prove to you, madame, that at my will I can cause you to be sad or joyful, cherished or neglected, adored or hated. Madame, listen to me: I love you."

"You insult me, monsieur!" cried the marquise, trying to withdraw the bridle of her horse from the abbe's hands.

"No fine words, my dear sister-in-law; for, with me, I warn you, they will be lost. To tell a woman one loves her is never an insult; only there are a thousand different ways of obliging her to respond to that love. The error is to make a mistake in the way that one employs—that is the whole of the matter."

"And may I inquire which you have chosen?" asked the marquise, with a crushing smile of contempt.

"The only one that could succeed with a calm, cold, strong woman like you, the conviction that your interest requires you to respond to my love."

"Since you profess to know me so well," answered the marquise, with another effort, as unsuccessful as the former, to free the bridle of her horse, "you should know how a woman like me would receive such an overture; say to yourself what I might say to you, and above all, what I might say to my husband."

The abbe smiled.

"Oh, as to that," he returned, "you can do as you please, madame. Tell your husband whatever you choose; repeat our conversation word for word; add whatever your memory may furnish, true or false, that may be most convincing against me; then, when you have thoroughly given him his cue, when you think yourself sure of him, I will say two words to him, and turn him inside out like this glove. That is what I had to say to you, madame I will not detain you longer. You may have in me a devoted friend or a mortal enemy. Reflect."

At these words the abbe loosed his hold upon the bridle of the marquise's horse and left her free to guide it as she would. The marquise put her beast to a trot, so as to show neither fear nor haste. The abbe followed her, and both rejoined the hunt.

The abbe had spoken truly. The marquise, notwithstanding the threat which she had made, reflected upon the influence which this man had over her husband, and of which she had often had proof she kept silence, therefore, and hoped that he had made himself seem worse than he was, to frighten her. On this point she was strangely mistaken.

The abbe, however, wished to see, in the first place, whether the marquise's refusal was due to personal antipathy or to real virtue. The chevalier, as has been said, was handsome; he had that usage of good society which does instead of mind, and he joined to it the obstinacy of a stupid man; the abbe undertook to persuade him that he was in love with the marquise. It was not a difficult matter. We have described the impression made upon the chevalier by the first sight of Madame de Ganges; but, owing beforehand the reputation of austerity that his sister-in-law had acquired, he had not the remotest idea of paying court to her. Yielding, indeed, to the influence which she exercised upon all who came in contact with her, the chevalier had remained her devoted servant; and the marquise, having no reason to mistrust civilities which she took for signs of friendliness, and considering his position as her husband's brother, treated him with less circumspection than was her custom.

The abbe sought him out, and, having made sure they were alone, said, "Chevalier, we both love the same woman, and that woman is our brother's wife; do not let us thwart each other: I am master of my passion, and can the more easily sacrifice it to you that I believe you are the man preferred; try, therefore, to obtain some assurance of the love which I suspect the marquise of having for you; and from the day when you reach that point I will withdraw, but otherwise, if you fail, give up your place civilly to me, that I may try, in my turn, whether her heart is really impregnable, as everybody says."

The chevalier had never thought of the possibility of winning the marquise; but from the moment in which his brother, with no apparent motive of personal interest, aroused the idea that he might be beloved, every spark of passion and of vanity that still existed in this automaton took fire, and he began to be doubly assiduous and attentive to his sister-in-law. She, who had never suspected any evil in this quarter, treated the chevalier at first with a kindliness that was heightened by her scorn for the abbe. But, before long, the chevalier, misunderstanding the grounds of this kindliness, explained himself more clearly. The marquise, amazed and at first incredulous, allowed him to say enough to make his intentions perfectly clear; then she stopped him, as she had done the abbe, by some of those galling words which women derive from their indifference even more than from their virtue.

At this check, the chevalier, who was far from possessing his brother's strength and determination, lost all hope, and came candidly to own to the latter the sad result of his attentions and his love. This was what the abbe had awaited, in the first place for the satisfaction of his own vanity, and in the second place for the means of carrying out his schemes. He worked upon the chevalier's humiliation until he had wrought it into a solid hatred; and then, sure of having him for a supporter and even for an accomplice, he began to put into execution his plan against the marquise.

The consequence was soon shown in a renewal of alienation on the part of M. de Ganges. A young man whom the marquise sometimes met in society, and to whom, on account of his wit, she listened perhaps a little more willingly than to others, became, if not the cause, at least the excuse of a fresh burst of jealousy. This jealousy was exhibited as on previous occasions, by quarrels remote from the real grievance; but the marquise was not deceived: she recognised in this change the fatal hand of her brother-in-law. But this certainty, instead of drawing her towards him, increased her repulsion; and thenceforward she lost no opportunity of showing him not only that repulsion but also the contempt that accompanied it.

Matters remained in this state for some months. Every day the marquise perceived her husband growing colder, and although the spies were invisible she felt herself surrounded by a watchfulness that took note of the most private details of her life. As to the abbe and the chevalier, they were as usual; only the abbe had hidden his hate behind a smile that was habitual, and the chevalier his resentment behind that cold and stiff dignity in which dull minds enfold themselves when they believe themselves injured in their vanity.

In the midst of all this, M. Joannis de Nocheres died, and added to the already considerable fortune of his granddaughter another fortune of from six to seven hundred thousand livres.

This additional wealth became, on accruing to the marquise, what was then called, in countries where the Roman law prevailed, a 'paraphernal' estate that is to say that, falling in, after marriage? it was not included in the dowry brought by the wife, and that she could dispose freely both of the capital and the income, which might not be administered even by her husband without a power of attorney, and of which she could dispose at pleasure, by donation or by will. And in fact, a few days after the marquise had entered into possession of her grandfather's estate, her husband and his brothers learned that she had sent for a notary in order to be instructed as to her rights. This step betokened an intention of separating this inheritance from the common property of the marriage; for the behaviour of the marquis towards his wife — of which within himself he often recognised the injustice — left him little hope of any other explanation.

About this time a strange event happened. At a dinner given by the marquise, a cream was served at dessert: all those who partook of this cream were ill; the marquis and his two brothers, who had not touched it, felt no evil effects. The remainder of this cream, which was suspected of having caused illness to the guests, and particularly to the marquise, who had taken of it twice, was analysed, and the presence of arsenic in it demonstrated. Only, having been mixed with milk, which is its antidote, the poison had lost some of its power, and had produced but half the expected effect. As no serious disaster had followed this occurrence, the blame was thrown upon a servant, who was said to have mistaken arsenic for sugar, and everybody forgot it, or appeared to forget it.

The marquis, however, seemed to be gradually and naturally drawing nearer again to his wife; but this time Madame de Ganges was not deceived by his returning kindness. There, as in his alienation, she saw the selfish hand of the abbe: he had persuaded his brother that seven hundred thousand livres more in the house would make it worth while to overlook some levities of behaviour; and the marquis, obeying the impulse given, was trying, by kind dealing, to oppose his wife's still unsettled intention of making a will.

Towards the autumn there was talk of going to spend that season at Ganges, a little town situated in Lower Languedoc, in the diocese of Montpellier, seven leagues from that town, and nineteen from Avignon. Although this was natural enough, since the marquis was lord of the town and had a castle there, the marquise was seized by a strange shudder when she heard the proposal. Remembrance of the prediction made to her returned immediately to her mind. The recent and ill explained attempt to poison her, too, very naturally added to her fears.

Without directly and positively suspecting her brothers-in-law of that crime, she knew that in them she had two implacable enemies. This journey to a little town, this abode in a lonely castle, amid new, unknown neighbours, seemed to her of no good omen; but open opposition would have been ridiculous. On what grounds, indeed, could she base resistance? The marquise could only own her terrors by accusing her husband and her brothers-in-law. And of what could she accuse them? The incident of the poisoned cream was not a conclusive proof. She resolved accordingly to lock up all her fears in her heart, and to commit herself to the hands of God.

Nevertheless, she would not leave Avignon without signing the will which she had contemplated making ever since M. de Nocheres' death. A notary was called in who drew up the document. The Marquise de Ganges made her mother, Madame de Rossan, her sole inheritor, and left in her charge the duty of choosing between the testatrix's two children as to which of them should succeed to the estate. These two children were, one a boy of six years old, the other a girl of five. But this was not enough for the marquise, so deep was her impression that she would not survive this fatal journey; she gathered together, secretly and at night, the magistrates of Avignon and several persons of quality, belonging to the first families of the town, and there, before them, verbally at first, declared that, in case of her death, she begged the honourable witnesses whom she had assembled on purpose, not to recognise as valid, voluntary, or freely written anything except the will which she had signed the day before, and affirmed beforehand that any later will which might be produced would be the effect of fraud or of violence. Then, having made this verbal declaration, the marquise repeated it in writing, signed the paper containing it, and gave the paper to be preserved by the honour of those whom she constituted its guardians. Such a precaution, taken with such minute detail, aroused the lively curiosity of her hearers. Many pressing questions were put to the marquise, but nothing could be extracted from her except that she had reasons for her action which she could not declare. The cause of this assemblage remained a secret, and every person who formed part of it promised the marquise not to reveal it.

On the next day, which was that preceding her departure for Ganges, the marquise visited all the charitable institutions and religious communities in Avignon; she left liberal alms everywhere, with the request that prayers and masses should be said for her, in order to obtain from God's grace that she should not be suffered to die without receiving the sacraments of the Church. In the evening, she took leave of all her friends with the affection and the tears of a person convinced that she was bidding them a last farewell; and finally she spent the whole night in prayer, and the maid who came to wake her found her kneeling in the same spot where she, had left her the night before.

The family set out for Ganges; the journey was performed without accident. On reaching the castle, the marquise found her mother-in-law there; she was a woman of remarkable distinction and piety, and her presence, although it was to be but temporary, reassured the poor fearful marquise a little. Arrangements had been made beforehand at the old castle, and the most convenient and elegant of the rooms had been assigned to the marquise; it was on the first floor, and looked out upon a courtyard shut in on all sides by stables.

On the first evening that she was to sleep here, the marquise explored the room with the greatest attention. She inspected the cupboards, sounded the walls, examined the tapestry, and found nothing anywhere that could confirm her terrors, which, indeed, from that time began to decrease. At the end of a certain time; however, the marquis's mother left Ganges to return to Montpellier. Two, days after her departure, the marquis talked of important business which required him to go back to Avignon, and he too left the castle. The marquise thus remained alone with the abbe, the chevalier, and a chaplain named Perette, who had been attached for five-and-twenty years to the family of the marquis. The rest of the household consisted of a few servants.

The marquise's first care, on arriving at the castle, had been to collect a little society for herself in the town. This was easy: not only did her rank make it an honour to belong to her circle, her kindly graciousness also inspired at first-sight the desire of having her for a friend. The marquise thus endured less dulness than she had at first feared. This precaution was by no means uncalled for; instead of spending only the autumn at Ganges, the marquise was obliged, in consequence of letters from her husband, to spend the winter there. During the whole of this time the abbe and the chevalier scemed to have completely forgotten their original designs upon her, and had again resumed the conduct of respectful, attentive brothers. But with all this, M. de Ganges remained estranged, and the marquise, who had not ceased to love him, though she began to lose her fear, did not lose her grief.

One day the abbe entered her room suddenly enough to surprise her before she had time to dry her tears; the secret being thus half surprised, he easily obtained a knowledge of the whole. The marquise owned to him that happiness in this world was impossible for her so long as her husband led this separate and hostile life. The abbe tried to console her; but amid his consolations he told her that the grief which she was suffering had its source in herself; that her husband was naturally wounded by her distrust of him—a distrust of which the will, executed by her, was a proof, all the more humiliating because public, and that, while that will existed, she could expect no advances towards reconciliation from her husband. For that time the conversation ended there.

Some days later, the abbe came into the marquise's room with a letter which he had just received from his brother. This letter, supposed confidential, was filled with tender complaints of his wife's conduct towards him, and showed, through every sentence, a depth of affection which only wrongs as serious as those from which the marquis considered himself to be feeling could counterbalance. The marquise was, at first, very much touched by this letter; but having soon reflected that just sufficient time had elapsed since the explanation between herself and the abbe for the marquis to be informed of it, she awaited further and stronger proofs before changing her mind.

From day to day, however, the abbe, under the pretext of reconciling the husband and wife, became more pressing upon the matter of the will, and the marquise, to whom this insistence seemed rather alarming, began to experience some of her former fears. Finally, the abbe pressed her so hard as to make her reflect that since, after the precautions which she had taken at Avignon, a revocation could have no result, it would be better to seem to yield rather than irritate this man, who inspired her with so great a fear, by constant and obstinate refusals. The next time that he returned to the subject she accordingly replied that she was ready to offer her husband this new proof of her love if it would bring him back to her, and having ordered a notary to be sent for, she made a new will, in the presence of the abbe and the chevalier, and constituted the marquis her residuary legatee. This second instrument bore date the 5th of May 1667. The abbe and the chevalier expressed the greatest joy that this subject of discord was at last removed, and offered themselves as guarantees, on their brother's behalf, of a better future. Some days were passed in this hope, which a letter from the marquis came to confirm; this letter at the same time announced his speedy return to Ganges.

On the 16th of May; the marquise, who for a month or two had not been well, determined to take medicine; she therefore informed the chemist of what she wanted, and asked him to make her up something at his discretion and send it to her the next day. Accordingly, at the agreed hour in the morning, the draught was brought to the marquise; but it looked to her so black and so thick that she felt some doubt of the skill of its compounder, shut it up in a cupboard in her room without saying anything of the matter, and took from her dressing-case some pills, of a less efficacious nature indeed, but to which she was accustomed, and which were not so repugnant to her.

The hour in which the marquise was to take this medicine was hardly over when the abbe and the chevalier sent to know how she was. She replied that she was quite well, and invited them to a collation which she was giving about four o'clock to the ladies who made up her little circle. An hour afterwards the abbe and the chevalier sent a second time to inquire after her; the marquise, without paying particular attention to this excessive civility, which she remembered afterwards, sent word as before that she was perfectly well. The marquise had remained in bed to do the honours of her little feast, and never had she felt more cheerful. At the hour named all her guests arrived; the abbe and the chevalier were ushered in, and the meal was served. Neither one nor the other would share it; the abbe indeed sat down to table, but the chevalier remained leaning on the foot of the bed. The abbe appeared anxious, and only roused himself with a start from his absorption; then he seemed to drive away some dominant idea, but soon the idea, stronger than his will, plunged him again into a reverie, a state which struck everyone the more particularly because it was far from his usual temper. As to the chevalier, his eyes were fixed constantly upon his sister-in-law, but in this there was not, as in his brother's behaviour, anything surprising, since the marquise had never looked so beautiful.

The meal over, the company took leave. The abbe escorted the ladies downstairs; the chevalier remained with the marquise; but hardly had the abbe left the room when Madame de Ganges saw the chevalier turn pale and drop in a sitting position—he had been standing on the foot of the bed. The marquise, uneasy, asked what was the matter; but before he could reply, her attention was called to another quarter. The abbe, as pale and as disturbed as the chevalier, came back into the room, carrying in his hands a glass and a pistol, and double-locked the door behind him. Terrified at this spectacle, the marquise half raised herself in her bed, gazing voiceless and wordless. Then the abbe approached her, his lips trembling; his hair bristling and his eyes blazing, and, presenting to her the glass and the pistol, "Madame," said he, after a moment of terrible silence, "choose, whether poison, fire, or"—he made a sign to the chevalier, who drew his sword—"or steel."

The marquise had one moment's hope: at the motion which she saw the chevalier make she thought he was coming to her assistance; but being soon undeceived, and finding herself between two men, both threatening her, she slipped from her bed and fell on her knees.

"What have I done," she cried, "oh, my God? that you should thus decree my death, and after having made yourselves judges should make

yourselves executioners? I am guilty of no fault towards you except of
having been too faithful in my duty to my husband, who is your brother."

Then seeing that it was vain to continue imploring the abbe, whose
looks and gestures spoke a mind made up, she turned towards the chevalier.

"And you too, brother," said she, "oh, God, God! you, too! Oh, have
pity on me, in the name of Heaven!"

But he, stamping his foot and pressing the point of his sword to her
bosom, answered—

"Enough, madam, enough; take your choice without delay; for if you do
not take it, we will take it for you."

The marquise turned once again to the abbe, and her forehead struck the
muzzle of the pistol. Then she saw that she must die indeed, and choosing
of the three forms of death that which seemed to her the least terrible, "Give
me the poison, then," said she, "and may God forgive you my death!"

With these words she took the glass, but the thick black liquid of
which it was full aroused such repulsion that she would have attempted
a last appeal; but a horrible imprecation from the abbe and a threatening
movement from his brother took from her the very last gleam of hope. She
put the glass to her lips, and murmuring once more, "God! Saviour! have
pity on me!" she swallowed the contents.

As she did so a few drops of the liquid fell upon her breast, and instantly
burned her skin like live coals; indeed, this infernal draught was composed
of arsenic and sublimate infused in aqua-fortis; then, thinking that no more
would be required of her, she dropped the glass.

The marquise was mistaken: the abbe picked it up, and observing that
all the sediment had remained at the bottom, he gathered together on a
silver bodkin all that had coagulated on the sides of the glass and all that
had sunk to the bottom, and presenting this ball, which was about the size
of a nut, to the marquise, on the end of the bodkin, he said, "Come, madame,
you must swallow the holy water sprinkler."

The marquise opened her lips, with resignation; but instead of doing as
the abbe commanded, she kept this remainder of the poison in her mouth,
threw herself on the bed with a scream, and clasping the pillows, in her pain,
she put out the poison between the sheets, unperceived by her assassins;
and then turning back to them, folded her hands in entreaty and said, "In
the name of God, since you have killed my body, at least do not destroy my
soul, but send me a confessor."

Cruel though the abbe and the chevalier were, they were no doubt beginning to weary of such a scene; moreover, the mortal deed was accomplished—after what she had drunk, the marquise could live but a few minutes; at her petition they went out, locking the door behind them. But no sooner did the marquise find herself alone than the possibility of flight presented itself to her. She ran to the window: this was but twenty-two feet above the ground, but the earth below was covered with stones and rubbish. The marquise, being only in her nightdress, hastened to slip on a silk petticoat; but at the moment when she finished tying it round her waist she heard a step approaching her room, and believing that her murderers were returning to make an end of her, she flew like a madwoman to the window. At the moment of her setting foot on the window ledge, the door opened: the marquise, ceasing to consider anything, flung herself down, head first.

Fortunately, the new-comer, who was the castle chaplain, had time to reach out and seize her skirt. The skirt, not strong enough to bear the weight of the marquise, tore; but its resistance, slight though it was, sufficed nevertheless to change the direction of her body: the marquise, whose head would have been shattered on the stones, fell on her feet instead, and beyond their being bruised by the stones, received no injury. Half stunned though she was by her fall, the marquise saw something coming after her, and sprang aside. It was an enormous pitcher of water, beneath which the priest, when he saw her escaping him, had tried to crush her; but either because he had ill carried out his attempt or because the marquise had really had time to move away, the vessel was shattered at her feet without touching her, and the priest, seeing that he had missed his aim, ran to warn the abbe and the chevalier that the victim was escaping.

As for the marquise, she had hardly touched the ground, when with admirable presence of mind she pushed the end of one of her long plaits so far down her throat as to provoke a fit of vomiting; this was the more easily done that she had eaten heartily of the collation, and happily the presence of the food had prevented the poison from attacking the coats of the stomach so violently as would otherwise have been the case. Scarcely had she vomited when a tame boar swallowed what she had rejected, and falling into a convulsion, died immediately.

As we have said, the room looked upon an enclosed courtyard; and the marquise at first thought that in leaping from her room into this court she had only changed her prison; but soon perceiving a light that flickered from an upper window of ore of the stables, she ran thither, and found a groom who was just going to bed.

"In the name of Heaven, my good man," said she to him, "save me! I am poisoned! They want to kill me! Do not desert me, I entreat you! Have pity on me, open this stable for me; let me get away! Let me escape!"

The groom did not understand much of what the marquise said to him; but seeing a woman with disordered hair, half naked, asking help of him, he took her by the arm, led her through the stables, opened a door for her, and the marquise found herself in the street. Two women were passing; the groom put her into their hands, without being able to explain to them what he did not know himself. As for the marquise, she seemed able to say nothing beyond these words: "Save me! I am poisoned! In the name of Heaven, save me!"

All at once she escaped from their hands and began to run like a mad woman; she had seen, twenty steps away, on the threshold of the door by which she had come, her two murderers in pursuit of her.

Then they rushed after her; she shrieking that she was poisoned, they shrieking that she was mad; and all this happening amid a crowd which, not knowing what part to take, divided and made way for the victim and the murderers. Terror gave the marquise superhuman strength: the woman who was accustomed to walk in silken shoes upon velvet carpets, ran with bare and bleeding feet over stocks and stones, vainly asking help, which none gave her; for, indeed, seeing her thus, in mad flight, in a nightdress, with flying hair, her only garment a tattered silk petticoat, it was difficult not to—think that this woman was, as her brothers-in-law said, mad.

At last the chevalier came up with her, stopped her, dragged her, in spite of her screams, into the nearest house, and closed the door behind them, while the abbe, standing at the threshold with a pistol in his hand, threatened to blow out the brains of any person who should approach.

The house into which the chevalier and the marquise had gone belonged to one M. Desprats, who at the moment was from home, and whose wife was entertaining several of her friends. The marquise and the chevalier, still struggling together, entered the room where the company was assembled: as among the ladies present were several who also visited the marquise, they immediately arose, in the greatest amazement, to give her the assistance that she implored; but the chevalier hastily pushed them aside, repeating that the marquise was mad. To this reiterated accusation—to which, indeed, appearances lent only too great a probability—the marquise replied by showing her burnt neck and her blackened lips, and wringing her hands in pain, cried out that she was poisoned, that she was going to die, and begged urgently for milk, or at least for water. Then the wife of a Protestant minister, whose name was Madame Brunel, slipped into her hand a box of orvietan, some pieces of which she hastened to swallow, while another lady gave her a glass of water; but at the instant when she was lifting it to her mouth, the chevalier broke it between her teeth, and one of the pieces of glass cut her lips. At this, all the women would have flung themselves upon the chevalier; but the marquise, fearing that he would only become more enraged, and hoping to disarm him, asked, on the contrary, that she might be left alone with him: all the company, yielding to her desire, passed into the next room; this was what the chevalier, on his part, too, asked.

Scarcely were they alone, when the marquise, joining her hands, knelt to him and said in the gentlest and most appealing voice that it was possible to use, "Chevalier, my dear brother, will you not have pity upon me, who have always had so much affection for you, and who, even now, would give my blood for your service? You know that the things I am saying are not merely empty words; and yet how is it you are treating me, though I have not deserved it? And what will everyone say to such dealings? Ah, brother, what a great unhappiness is mine, to have been so cruelly treated by you! And yet—yes, brother—if you will deign to have pity on me and to save my life, I swear, by my hope of heaven, to keep no remembrance of what has happened; and to consider you always as my protector and my friend."

All at once the marquise rose with a great cry and clasped her hand to her right side. While she was speaking, and before she perceived what he was doing, the chevalier had drawn his sword, which was very short, and using it as a dagger, had struck her in the breast; this first blow was followed by a second, which came in contact with the shoulder blade, and so was prevented from going farther. At these two blows the marquise rushed towards the door, of the room into which the ladies had retired, crying, "Help! He is killing me!"

But during the time that she took to cross the room the chevalier stabbed her five times in the back with his sword, and would no doubt have done more, if at the last blow his sword had not broken; indeed, he had struck with such force that the fragment remained embedded in her shoulder, and the marquise fell forward on the floor, in a pool of her blood, which was flowing all round her and spreading through the room.

The chevalier thought he had killed her, and hearing the women running to her assistance, he rushed from the room. The abbe was still at the door, pistol in hand; the chevalier took him by the arm to drag him away, and as the abbe hesitated to follow, he said:—

"Let us go, abbe; the business is done."

The chevalier and the abbe had taken a few steps in the street when a window opened and the women who had found the marquise expiring called out for help: at these cries the abbe stopped short, and holding back the chevalier by the arm, demanded—

"What was it you said, chevalier? If they are calling help, is she not dead, after all?"

"'Ma foi', go and see for yourself," returned the chevalier. "I have done enough for my share; it is your turn now."

"'Pardieu', that is quite my opinion," cried the abbe; and rushing back to the house, he flung himself into the room at the moment when the women, lifting the marquise with great difficulty, for she was so weak that she could no longer help herself, were attempting to carry her to bed. The abbe pushed them away, and arriving at the marquise, put his pistol to her heart; but Madame Brunel, the same who had previously given the marquise a box of orvietan, lifted up the barrel with her hand, so that the shot went off into the air, and the bullet instead of striking the marquise lodged in the cornice of the ceiling. The abbe then took the pistol by the barrel and gave Madame Brunet so violent a blow upon the head with the butt that she staggered and almost fell; he was about to strike her again, but all the women uniting against him, pushed him, with thousands of maledictions, out of the room, and locked the door behind him. The two assassins, taking advantage of the darkness, fled from Ganges, and reached Aubenas, which is a full league away, about ten in the evening.

Meanwhile the women were doing all they could for the marquise. Their first intention, as we have already said, was to put her to bed, but the broken sword blade made her unable to lie down, and they tried in vain to pull it out, so deeply had it entered the bone. Then the marquise herself showed Madame Brunei what method to take: the operating lady was to sit on the bed, and while the others helped to hold up the marquise, was to seize the blade with both hands, and pressing her—knees against the patient's back, to pull violently and with a great jerk. This plan at last succeeded, and the marquise was able to get to bed; it was nine in the evening, and this horrible tragedy had been going on for nearly three hours.

The magistrates of Ganges, being informed of what had happened, and beginning to believe that it was really a case of murder, came in person, with a guard, to the marquise. As soon as she saw them come in she recovered strength, and raising herself in bed, so great was her fear, clasped her hands and besought their protection; for she always expected to see one or the other of her murderers return. The magistrates told her to reassure herself, set armed men to guard all the approaches to the house, and while physicians and surgeons were, summoned in hot haste from Montpellier, they on their part sent word to the Baron de Trissan, provost of Languedoc, of the crime that had just been committed, and gave him the names and the description of the murderers. That official at once sent people after them, but it was already too late: he learned that the abbe and the chevalier had slept at Aubenas on the night of the murder, that there they had reproached each other for their unskilfulness, and had come near cutting each other's throats, that finally they had departed before daylight, and had taken a boat, near Agde, from a beach called the "Gras de Palaval."

The Marquis de Ganges was at Avignon, where he was prosecuting a servant of his who had robbed him of two hundred crowns; when he heard news of the event. He turned horribly pale as he listened to the messenger's story, then falling into a violent fury against his brothers, he swore that they should have no executioners other than himself. Nevertheless, though he was so uneasy about the marquise's condition, he waited until the next day in the afternoon before setting forth, and during the interval he saw some of his friends at Avignon without saying anything to them of the matter. He did not reach Ganges until four days after the murder, then he went to the house of M. Desprats and asked to see his wife, whom some kind priests had already prepared for the meeting; and the marquise, as soon as she heard of his arrival, consented to receive him. The marquis immediately entered the room, with his eyes full of tears, tearing his hair, and giving every token of the deepest despair.

The marquise receivers her husband like a forgiving wife and a dying Christian. She scarcely even uttered some slight reproaches about the manner in which he had deserted her; moreover, the marquis having complained to a monk of these reproaches, and the monk having reported his complaints to the marquise, she called her husband to her bedside, at a moment when she was surrounded by people, and made him a public apology, begging him to attribute the words that seemed to have wounded him to the effect of her sufferings, and not to any failure in her regard for him. The marquis, left alone with his wife, tried to take advantage of this reconciliation to induce her to annul the declaration that she had made before the magistrates of Avignon; for the vice-legate and his officers, faithful to the promises made to the marquise, had refused to register the fresh donation which she had made at Ganges, according to the suggestions of the abbe, and which the latter had sent off, the very moment it was signed, to his brother. But on this point the marquise was immovably resolute, declaring that this fortune was reserved for her children and therefore sacred to her, and that she could make no alteration in what had been done at Avignon, since it represented her genuine and final wishes. Notwithstanding this declaration, the marquis did not cease to—remain beside his wife and to bestow upon her every care possible to a devoted and attentive husband.

Two days later than the Marquis de Ganges arrived Madame de Rossan great was her amazement, after all the rumours that were already in circulation about the marquis, at finding her daughter in the hands of him whom she regarded as one of her murderers. But the marquise, far from sharing that opinion, did all she could, not only to make her mother feel differently, but even to induce her to embrace the marquis as a son. This blindness on the part of the marquise caused Madame de Rossan so much grief that notwithstanding her profound affection for her daughter she would only stay two days, and in spite of the entreaties that the dying woman made to her, she returned home, not allowing anything to stop her. This departure was a great grief to the marquise, and was the reason why she begged with renewed entreaties to be taken to Montpellier. The very sight of the place where she had been so cruelly tortured continually brought before her, not only the remembrance of the murder, but the image of the murderers, who in her brief moments of sleep so haunted her that she sometimes awoke suddenly, uttering shrieks and calling for help. Unfortunately, the physician considered her too weak to bear removal, and declared that no change of place could be made without extreme danger.

Then, when she heard this verdict, which had to be repeated to her, and which her bright and lively complexion and brilliant eyes seemed to contradict, the marquise turned all her thoughts towards holy things, and thought only of dying like a saint after having already suffered like a martyr. She consequently asked to receive the last sacrament, and while it was being sent for, she repeated her apologies to her husband and her forgiveness of his brothers, and this with a gentleness that, joined to her beauty, made her whole personality appear angelic. When, however, the priest bearing the viaticum entered, this expression suddenly changed, and her face presented every token of the greatest terror. She had just recognised in the priest who was bringing her the last consolations of Heaven the infamous Perette, whom she could not but regard as an accomplice of the abbe and the chevalier, since, after having tried to hold her back, he had attempted to crush her beneath the pitcher of water which he had thrown at her from the window, and since, when he saw her escaping, he had run to warn her assassins and to set them on her track. She recovered herself quickly, however, and seeing that the priest, without any sign of remorse, was drawing near to her bedside, she would not cause so great a scandal as would have been caused by denouncing him at such a moment. Nevertheless, bending towards him, she said, "Father, I hope that, remembering what has passed, and in order to dispel fears that—I may justifiably entertain, you will make no difficulty of partaking with me of the consecrated wafer; for I have sometimes heard it said that the body of our Lord Jesus Christ, while remaining a token of salvation, has been known to be made a principle of death."

The priest inclined his head as a sign of assent.

So the marquise communicated thus, taking a sacrament that she shared with one of her murderers, as an evidence that she forgave this one like the others and that she prayed God to forgive them as she herself did.

The following days passed without any apparent increase in her illness, the fever by which she was consumed rather enhancing her beauties, and imparting to her voice and gestures a vivacity which they had never had before. Thus everybody had begun to recover hope, except herself, who, feeling better than anyone else what was her true condition, never for a moment allowed herself any illusion, and keeping her son, who was seven years old, constantly beside her bed, bade him again and again look well at her, so that, young as he was, he might remember her all his life and never forget her in his prayers. The poor child would burst into tears and promise not only to remember her but also to avenge her when he was a man. At these words the marquise gently reproved him, telling him that all vengeance belonged to the king and to God, and that all cares of the kind must be left to those two great rulers of heaven and of earth.

On the 3rd of June, M. Catalan, a councillor, appointed as a commissioner by the Parliament of Toulouse, arrived at Ganges, together with all the officials required by his commission; but he could not see the marquise that night, for she had dozed for some hours, and this sleep had left a sort of torpor upon her mind, which might have impaired the lucidity of her depositions. The next morning, without asking anybody's opinion, M. Catalan repaired to the house of M. Desprats, and in spite of some slight resistance on the part of those who were in charge of her, made his way to the presence of the marquise. The dying woman received him with an admirable presence of mind, that made M. Catalan think there had been an intention the night before to prevent any meeting between him and the person whom he was sent to interrogate. At first the marquise would relate nothing that had passed, saying that she could not at the same time accuse and forgive; but M. Catalan brought her to see that justice required truth from her before all things, since, in default of exact information, the law might go astray, and strike the innocent instead of the guilty. This last argument decided the marquise, and during the hour and a half that he spent alone with her she told him all the details of this horrible occurrence. On the morrow M. Catalan was to see her again; but on the morrow the marquise was, in truth, much worse. He assured himself of this by his own eyes, and as he knew almost all that he wished to know, did not insist further, for fear of fatiguing her.

Indeed, from that day forward, such atrocious sufferings laid hold upon the marquise, that notwithstanding the firmness which she had always shown, and which she tried to maintain to the end, she could not prevent herself from uttering screams mingled with prayers. In this manner she spent the whole day of the 4th and part of the 5th. At last, on that day, which was a Sunday, towards four o'clock in the afternoon, she expired.

The body was immediately opened, and the physicians attested that the marquise had died solely from the power of the poison, none of the seven sword cuts which she had received being, mortal. They found the stomach and bowels burned and the brain blackened. However, in spite of that infernal draught, which, says the official report, "would have killed a lioness in a few hours," the marquise struggled for nineteen days, so much, adds an account from which we have borrowed some of these details, so much did nature lovingly defend the beautiful body that she had taken so much trouble to make.

A. Catalan, the very moment he was informed of the marquise's death, having with him twelve guards belonging to the governor, ten archers, and a poqueton,—despatched them to the marquis's castle with orders to seize his person, that of the priest, and those of all the servants except the groom who had assisted the marquise in her flight. The officer in command of this little squad found the marquis walking up and down, melancholy and greatly disturbed, in the large hall of the castle, and when he signified to him the order of which he was the bearer, the marquis, without making any resistance, and as though prepared for what was happening to him, replied that he was ready to obey, and that moreover he had always intended to go before the Parliament to accuse the murderers of his wife. He was asked for the key of his cabinet, which he gave up, and the order was given to conduct him, with the other persons accused, to the prisons of Montpellier. As soon as the marquis came into that town, the report of his arrival spread with incredible rapidity from street to street. Then, as it was dark, lights came to all the windows, and people corning out with torches formed a torchlight procession, by means of which everybody could see him. He, like the priest, was mounted on a sorry hired horse, and entirely surrounded by archers, to whom, no doubt, he owed his life on this occasion; for the indignation against him was so great that everyone was egging on his neighbours to tear him limb from limb, which would certainly have come to pass had he not been so carefully defended and guarded.

Immediately upon receiving news of her daughter's death, Madame de Rossan took possession of all her property, and, making herself a party to the case, declared that she would never desist from her suit until her daughter's death was avenged. M. Catalan began the examination at once, and the first interrogation to which he submitted the marquis lasted eleven hours. Then soon afterwards he and the other persons accused were conveyed from the prisons of Montpellier to those of Toulouse. A crushing memorial by Madame de Rossan followed them, in which she demonstrated with absolute clearness that the marquis had participated in the crime of his two brothers, if not in act, in thought, desire, and intention.

The marquis's defence was very simple: it was his misfortune to have had two villains for brothers, who had made attempts first upon the honour and then upon the life of a wife whom he loved tenderly; they had destroyed her by a most atrocious death, and to crown his evil fortune, he, the innocent, was accused of having had a hand in that death. And, indeed, the examinations in the trial did not succeed in bringing any evidence against the marquis beyond moral presumptions, which, it appears, were insufficient to induce his judges to award a sentence of death.

A verdict was consequently given, upon the 21st of August, 1667, which sentenced the abbe and the chevalier de Ganges to be broken alive on the wheel, the Marquis de Ganges to perpetual banishment from the kingdom, his property to be confiscated to the king, and himself to lose his nobility and to become incapable of succeeding to the property of his children. As for the priest Perette, he was sentenced to the galleys for life, after having previously been degraded from his clerical orders by the ecclesiastical authorities.

This sentence made as great a stir as the murder had done, and gave rise, in that period when "extenuating circumstances" had not been invented, to long and angry discussions. Indeed, the marquis either was guilty of complicity or was not: if he was not, the punishment was too cruel; if he was, the sentence was too light. Such was the opinion of Louis XIV., who remembered the beauty of the Marquis de Ganges; for, some time afterwards, when he was believed to have forgotten this unhappy affair, and when he was asked to pardon the Marquis de la Douze, who was accused of having poisoned his wife, the king answered, "There is no need for a pardon, since he belongs to the Parliament of Toulouse, and the Marquis de Ganges did very well without one."

It may easily be supposed that this melancholy event did not pass without inciting the wits of the day to write a vast number of verses and bouts-rimes about the catastrophe by which one of the most beautiful women of the country was carried off. Readers who have a taste for that sort of literature are referred to the journals and memoirs of the times.

Now, as our readers, if they have taken any interest at all in the terrible tale just narrated, will certainly ask what became of the murderers, we will proceed to follow their course until the moment when they disappeared, some into the night of death, some into the darkness of oblivion.

The priest Perette was the first to pay his debt to Heaven: he died at the oar on the way from Toulouse to Brest.

The chevalier withdrew to Venice, took service in the army of the Most Serene Republic, then at war with Turkey, and was sent to Candia, which the Mussulmans had been besieging for twenty years; he had scarcely arrived there when, as he was walking on the ramparts of the town with two other officers, a shell burst at their feet, and a fragment of it killed the chevalier without so much as touching his companions, so that the event was regarded as a direct act of Providence.

As for the abbe, his story is longer and stranger. He parted from the chevalier in the neighbourhood of Genoa, and crossing the whole of Piedmont, part of Switzerland, and a corner of Germany, entered Holland under the name of Lamartelliere. After many hesitations as to the place where he would settle, he finally retired to Viane, of which the Count of Lippe was at that time sovereign; there he made the acquaintance of a gentleman who presented him to the count as a French religious refugee.

The count, even in this first conversation, found that the foreigner who had come to seek safety in his dominions possessed not only great intelligence but a very solid sort of intelligence, and seeing that the Frenchman was conversant with letters and with learning, proposed that he should undertake the education of his son, who at that time was nine years old. Such a proposal was a stroke of fortune for the abbe de Ganges, and he did not dream of refusing it.

The abbe de Ganges was one of those men who have great mastery over themselves: from the moment when he saw that his interest, nay, the very safety of his life required it, he concealed with extreme care whatever bad passions existed within him, and only allowed his good qualities to appear. He was a tutor who supervised the heart as sharply as the mind, and succeeded in making of his pupil a prince so accomplished in both respects, that the Count of Lippe, making use of such wisdom and such knowledge, began to consult the tutor upon all matters of State, so that in course of time the so-called Lamartelliere, without holding any public office, had become the soul of the little principality.

The countess had a young relation living with her, who though without fortune was of a great family, and for whom the countess had a deep affection; it did not escape her notice that her son's tutor had inspired this poor young girl with warmer feelings than became her high station, and that the false Lamartelliere, emboldened by his own growing credit, had done all he could to arouse and keep up these feelings. The countess sent for her cousin, and having drawn from her a confession of her love, said that she herself had indeed a great regard for her son's governor, whom she and her husband intended to reward with pensions and with posts for the services he had rendered to their family and to the State, but that it was too lofty an ambition for a man whose name was Lamartelliere, and who had no relations nor family that could be owned, to aspire to the hand of a girl who was related to a royal house; and that though she did not require that the man who married her cousin should be a Bourbon, a Montmorency, or a Rohan, she did at least desire that he should be somebody, though it were but a gentleman of Gascony or Poitou.

The Countess of Lippe's young kinswoman went and repeated this answer, word for word, to her lover, expecting him to be overwhelmed by it; but, on the contrary, he replied that if his birth was the only obstacle that opposed their union, there might be means to remove it. In fact, the abbe, having spent eight years at the prince's court, amid the strongest testimonies of confidence and esteem, thought himself sure enough of the prince's goodwill to venture upon the avowal of his real name.

He therefore asked an audience of the countess, who immediately granted it. Bowing to her respectfully, he said, "Madame, I had flattered myself that your Highness honoured me with your esteem, and yet you now oppose my happiness: your Highness's relative is willing to accept me as a husband, and the prince your son authorises my wishes and pardons my boldness; what have I done to you, madame, that you alone should be against me? and with what can you reproach me during the eight years that I have had the honour of serving your Highness?"

"I have nothing to reproach you with, monsieur," replied the countess: "but I do not wish to incur reproach on my own part by permitting such a marriage: I thought you too sensible and reasonable a man to need reminding that, while you confined yourself to suitable requests and moderate ambitions, you had reason to be pleased with our gratitude. Do you ask that your salary shall be doubled? The thing is easy. Do you desire important posts? They shall be given you; but do not, sir, so far forget yourself as to aspire to an alliance that you cannot flatter yourself with a hope of ever attaining."

"But, madame," returned the petitioner, "who told you that my birth was so obscure as to debar me from all hope of obtaining your consent?"

"Why, you yourself, monsieur, I think," answered the countess in astonishment; "or if you did not say so, your name said so for you."

"And if that name is not mine, madame?" said the abbe, growing bolder; "if unfortunate, terrible, fatal circumstances have compelled me to take that name in order to hide another that was too unhappily famous, would your Highness then be so unjust as not to change your mind?"

"Monsieur," replied the countess, "you have said too much now not to go on to the end. Who are you? Tell me. And if, as you give me to understand, you are of good birth, I swear to you that want of fortune shall not stand in the way."

"Alas, madame," cried the abbe, throwing himself at her feet, "my name, I am sure, is but too familiar to your Highness, and I would willingly at this moment give half my blood that you had never heard it uttered; but you have said it, madame, have gone too far to recede. Well, then, I am that unhappy abbe de Ganges whose crimes are known and of whom I have more than once heard you speak."

"The abbe de Ganges!" cried the countess in horror,—"the abbe de Ganges! You are that execrable abbe de Ganges whose very name makes one shudder? And to you, to a man thus infamous, we have entrusted the education of our only son? Oh, I hope, for all our sakes, monsieur, that you are speaking falsely; for if you were speaking the truth I think I should have you arrested this very instant and taken back to France to undergo your punishment. The best thing you can do, if what you have said to me is true, is instantly to leave not only the castle, but the town and the principality; it will be torment enough for the rest of my life whenever I think that I have spent seven years under the same roof with you."

The abbe would have replied; but the countess raised her voice so much, that the young prince, who had been won over to his tutor's interests and who was listening at his mother's door, judged that his protege's business was taking an unfavourable turn; and went in to try and put things right. He found his mother so much alarmed that she drew him to her by an instinctive movement, as though to put herself under his protection, and beg and pray as he might; he could only obtain permission for his tutor to go away undisturbed to any country of the world that he might prefer, but with an express prohibition of ever again entering the presence of the Count or the Countess of Lippe.

The abbe de Ganges withdrew to Amsterdam, where he became a teacher of languages, and where his lady-love soon after came to him and married him: his pupil, whom his parents could not induce, even when they told him the real name of the false Lamartelliere, to share their horror of him, gave him assistance as long as he needed it; and this state of things continued until upon his wife attaining her majority he entered into possession of some property that belonged to her. His regular conduct and his learning, which had been rendered more solid by long and serious study, caused him to be admitted into the Protestant consistory; there, after an exemplary life, he died, and none but God ever knew whether it was one of hypocrisy or of penitence.

As for the Marquis de Ganges, who had been sentenced, as we have seen, to banishment and the confiscation of his property, he was conducted to the frontier of Savoy and there set at liberty. After having spent two or three years abroad, so that the terrible catastrophe in which he had been concerned should have time to be hushed up, he came back to France, and as nobody—Madame de Rossan being now dead—was interested in prosecuting him, he returned to his castle at Ganges, and remained there, pretty well hidden. M. de Baville, indeed, the Lieutenant of Languedoc, learned that the marquis had broken from his exile; but he was told, at the same time, that the marquis, as a zealous Catholic, was forcing his vassals to attend mass, whatever their religion might be: this was the period in which persons of the Reformed Church were being persecuted, and the zeal of the marquis appeared to M. de Baville to compensate and more than compensate for the peccadillo of which he had been accused; consequently, instead of prosecuting him, he entered into secret communication with him, reassuring him about his stay in France, and urging on his religious zeal; and in this manner twelve years passed by.

During this time the marquise's young son, whom we saw at his mother's deathbed, had reached the age of twenty, and being rich in his father's possessions—which his uncle had restored to him—and also by his mother's inheritance, which he had shared with his sister, had married a girl of good family, named Mademoiselle de Moissac, who was both rich and beautiful. Being called to serve in the royal army, the count brought his young wife to the castle of Ganges, and, having fervently commended her to his father, left her in his charge.

The Marquis de Ganges was forty-two veers old, and scarcely seemed thirty; he was one of the handsomest men living; he fell in love with his daughter-in-law and hoped to win her love, and in order to promote this design, his first care was to separate from her, under the excuse of religion, a maid who had been with her from childhood and to whom she was greatly attached.

This measure, the cause of which the young marquise did not know, distressed her extremely. It was much against her will that she had come to live at all in this old castle of Ganges, which had so recently been the scene of the terrible story that we have just told. She inhabited the suite of rooms in which the murder had been committed; her bedchamber was the same which had belonged to the late marquise; her bed was the same; the window by which she had fled was before her eyes; and everything, down to the smallest article of furniture, recalled to her the details of that savage tragedy. But even worse was her case when she found it no longer possible to doubt her father-in-law's intentions; when she saw herself beloved by one whose very name had again and again made her childhood turn pale with terror, and when she was left alone at all hours of the day in the sole company of the man whom public rumour still pursued as a murderer. Perhaps in any other place the poor lonely girl might have found some strength in trusting herself to God; but there, where God had suffered one of the fairest and purest creatures that ever existed to perish by so cruel a death, she dared not appeal to Him, for He seemed to have turned away from this family.

She waited, therefore, in growing terror; spending her days, as much as she could, with the women of rank who lived in the little town of Ganges, and some of whom, eye-witnesses of her mother-in-law's murder, increased her terrors by the accounts which they gave of it, and which she, with the despairing obstinacy of fear, asked to hear again and again. As to her nights, she spent the greater part of them on her knees, and fully dressed, trembling at the smallest sound; only breathing freely as daylight came back, and then venturing to seek her bed for a few hours' rest.

At last the marquis's attempts became so direct and so pressing, that the poor young woman resolved to escape at all costs from his hands. Her first idea was to write to her father, explain to him her position and ask help; but her father had not long been a Catholic, and had suffered much on behalf of the Reformed religion, and on these accounts it was clear that her letter would be opened by the marquis on pretext of religion, and thus that step, instead of saving, might destroy her. She had thus but one resource: her husband had always been a Catholic; her husband was a captain of dragoons, faithful in the service of the king and faithful in the service of God; there could be no excuse for opening a letter to him; she resolved to address herself to him, explained the position in which she found herself, got the address written by another hand, and sent the letter to Montpellier, where it was posted.

The young marquis was at Metz when he received his wife's missive. At that instant all his childish memories awoke; he beheld himself at his dying mother's bedside, vowing never to forget her and to pray daily for her. The image presented itself of this wife whom he adored, in the same room, exposed to the same violence, destined perhaps to the same fate; all this was enough to lead him to take positive action: he flung himself into a post-chaise, reached Versailles, begged an audience of the king, cast himself, with his wife's letter in his hand, at the feet of Louis XIV, and besought him to compel his father to return into exile, where he swore upon has honour that he would send him everything he could need in order to live properly.

The king was not aware that the Marquis do Ganges had disobeyed the sentence of banishment, and the manner in which he learned it was not such as to make him pardon the contradiction of his laws. In consequence he immediately ordered that if the Marquis de Ganges were found in France he should be proceeded against with the utmost rigour.

Happily for the marquis, the Comte de Ganges, the only one of his brothers who had remained in France, and indeed in favour, learned the king's decision in time. He took post from Versailles, and making the greatest haste, went to warn him of the danger that was threatening; both together immediately left Ganges, and withdrew to Avignon. The district of Venaissin, still belonging at that time to the pope and being governed by a vice-legate, was considered as foreign territory. There he found his daughter, Madame d'Urban, who did all she could to induce him to stay with her; but to do so would have been to flout Louis XIV's orders too publicly, and the marquis was afraid to remain so much in evidence lest evil should befall him; he accordingly retired to the little village of l'Isle, built in a charming spot near the fountain of Vaucluse; there he was lost sight of; none ever heard him spoken of again, and when I myself travelled in the south of France in 1835, I sought in vain any trace of the obscure and forgotten death which closed so turbulent and stormy an existence.

As, in speaking of the last adventures of the Marquis de Ganges, we have mentioned the name of Madame d'Urban, his daughter, we cannot exempt ourselves from following her amid the strange events of her life, scandalous though they may be; such, indeed, was the fate of this family, that it was to occupy the attention of France through well-nigh a century, either by its crimes or by its freaks.

On the death of the marquise, her daughter, who was barely six years old, had remained in the charge of the dowager Marquise de Ganges, who, when she had attained her twelfth year, presented to her as her husband the Marquis de Perrant, formerly a lover of the grandmother herself. The marquis was seventy years of age, having been born in the reign of Henry IV; he had seen the court of Louis XIII and that of Louis XIV's youth, and he had remained one of its most elegant and favoured nobles; he had the manners of those two periods, the politest that the world has known, so that the young girl, not knowing as yet the meaning of marriage and having seen no other man, yielded without repugnance, and thought herself happy in becoming the Marquise de Perrant.

The marquis, who was very rich, had quarrelled With his younger brother, and regarded him with such hatred that he was marrying only to deprive his brother of the inheritance that would rightfully accrue to him, should the elder die childless. Unfortunately, the marquis soon perceived that the step which he had taken, however efficacious in the case of another man, was likely to be fruitless in his own. He did not, however, despair, and waited two or three years, hoping every day that Heaven would work a miracle in his favour; but as every day diminished the chances of this miracle, and his hatred for his brother grew with the impossibility of taking revenge upon him, he adopted a strange and altogether antique scheme, and determined, like the ancient Spartans, to obtain by the help of another what Heaven refused to himself.

The marquis did not need to seek long for the man who should give him his revenge: he had in his house a young page, some seventeen or eighteen years old, the son of a friend of his, who, dying without fortune, had on his deathbed particularly commended the lad to the marquis. This young man, a year older than his mistress, could not be continually about her without falling passionately in love with her; and however much he might endeavour to hide his love, the poor youth was as yet too little practised in dissimulation to succeed iii concealing it from the eyes of the marquis, who, after having at first observed its growth with uneasiness, began on the contrary to rejoice in it, from the moment when he had decided upon the scheme that we have just mentioned.

The marquis was slow to decide but prompt to execute. Having taken his resolution, he summoned his page, and, after having made him promise inviolable secrecy, and having undertaken, on that condition, to prove his gratitude by buying him a regiment, explained what was expected of him. The poor youth, to whom nothing could have been more unexpected than such a communication, took it at first for a trick by which the marquis meant to make him own his love, and was ready to throw himself at his feet and declare everything; but the marquis seeing his confusion, and easily guessing its cause, reassured him completely by swearing that he authorised him to take any steps in order to attain the end that the marquis had in view. As in his inmost heart the aim of the young man was the same, the bargain was soon struck: the page bound himself by the most terrible oaths to keep the secret; and the marquis, in order to supply whatever assistance was in his power, gave him money to spend, believing that there was no woman, however virtuous, who could resist the combination of youth, beauty, and fortune: unhappily for the marquis, such a woman, whom he thought impossible, did exist, and was his wife.

The page was so anxious to obey his master, that from that very day his mistress remarked the alteration that arose from the permission given him—his prompt obedience to her orders and his speed in executing them, in order to return a few moments the sooner to her presence. She was grateful to him, and in the simplicity of her heart she thanked him. Two days later the page appeared before her splendidly dressed; she observed and remarked upon his improved appearance, and amused herself in conning over all the parts of his dress, as she might have done with a new doll. All this familiarity doubled the poor young man's passion, but he stood before his mistress, nevertheless, abashed and trembling, like Cherubino before his fair godmother. Every evening the marquis inquired into his progress, and every evening the page confessed that he was no farther advanced than the day before; then the marquis scolded, threatened to take away his fine clothes, to withdraw his own promises, and finally to address himself to some other person. At this last threat the youth would again call up his courage, and promise to be bolder to-morrow; and on the morrow would spend the day in making a thousand compliments to his mistress's eyes, which she, in her innocence, did not understand. At last, one day, Madame de Perrant asked him what made him look at her thus, and he ventured to confess his love; but then Madame de Perrant, changing her whole demeanour, assumed a face of sternness and bade him go out of her room.

The poor lover obeyed, and ran, in despair, to confide his grief to the husband, who appeared sincerely to share it, but consoled him by saying that he had no doubt chosen his moment badly; that all women, even the least severe, had inauspicious hours in which they would not yield to attack, and that he must let a few days pass, which he must employ in making his peace, and then must take advantage of a better opportunity, and not allow himself to be rebuffed by a few refusals; and to these words the marquis added a purse of gold, in order that the page might, if necessary, win over the marquise's waiting-woman.

Guided thus by the older experience of the husband, the page began to appear very much ashamed and very penitent; but for a day or two the marquise, in spite of his apparent humility, kept him at a distance: at last, reflecting no doubt, with the assistance of her mirror and of her maid, that the crime was not absolutely unpardonable, and after having reprimanded the culprit at some length, while he stood listening with eyes cast down, she gave a him her hand, forgave him, and admitted him to her companionship as before.

Things went on in this way for a week. The page no longer raised his eyes and did not venture to open his mouth, and the marquise was beginning to regret the time in which he used to look and to speak, when, one fine day while she was at her toilet, at which she had allowed him to be present, he seized a moment when the maid had left her alone, to cast himself at her feet and tell her that he had vainly tried to stifle his love, and that, even although he were to die under the weight of her anger, he must tell her that this love was immense, eternal, stronger than his life. The marquise upon this wished to send him away, as on the former occasion, but instead of obeying her, the page, better instructed, took her in his arms. The marquise called, screamed, broke her bell-rope; the waiting-maid, who had been bought over, according to the marquis's advice, had kept the other women out of the way, and was careful not to come herself. Then the marquise, resisting force by force, freed herself from the page's arms, rushed to her husband's room, and there, bare-necked, with floating hair, and looking lovelier than ever, flung herself into his arms and begged his protection against the insolent fellow who had just insulted her. But what was the amazement of the marquise, when, instead of the anger which she expected to see break forth, the marquis answered coldly that what she was saying was incredible, that he had always found the young man very well behaved, and that, no doubt, having taken up some frivolous ground of resentment against him, she was employing this means to get rid of him; but, he added, whatever might be his love for her, and his desire to do everything that was agreeable to her, he begged her not to require this of him, the young man being his friend's son, and consequently his own adopted child. It was now the marquise who, in her turn, retired abashed, not knowing what to make of such a reply, and fully resolving, since her husband's protection failed her, to keep herself well guarded by her own severity.

Indeed, from that moment the marquise behaved to the poor youth with so much prudery, that, loving her as he did, sincerely, he would have died of grief, if he had not had the marquis at hand to encourage and strengthen him. Nevertheless, the latter himself began to despair, and to be more troubled by the virtue of his wife than another man might have been by the levity of his. Finally, he resolved, seeing that matters remained at the same point and that the marquise did not relax in the smallest degree, to take extreme measures. He hid his page in a closet of his wife's bedchamber, and, rising during her first sleep, left empty his own place beside her, went out softly, double-locked the door, and listened attentively to hear what would happen.

He had not been listening thus for ten minutes when he heard a great noise in the room, and the page trying in vain to appease it. The marquis hoped that he might succeed, but the noise increasing, showed him that he was again to be disappointed; soon came cries for help, for the marquise could not ring, the bell-ropes having been lifted out of her reach, and no one answering her cries, he heard her spring from her high bed, run to the door, and finding it locked rush to the window, which she tried to open: the scene had come to its climax.

The marquis decided to go in, lest some tragedy should happen, or lest his wife's screams should reach some belated passer-by, who next day would make him the talk of the town. Scarcely did the marquise behold him when she threw herself into his arms, and pointing to the page, said:—

"Well, monsieur, will you still hesitate to free me from this insolent wretch?"

"Yes, madame," replied the marquis; "for this insolent wretch has been acting for the last three months not only with my sanction but even by my orders."

The marquise remained stupefied. Then the marquis, without sending away the page, gave his wife an explanation of all that had passed, and besought her to yield to his desire of obtaining a successor, whom he would regard as his own child, so long as it was hers; but young though she was, the marquise answered with a dignity unusual at her age, that his power over her had the limits that were set to it by law, and not those that it might please him to set in their place, and that however much she might wish to do what might be his pleasure, she would yet never obey him at the expense of her soul and her honour.

So positive an answer, while it filled her husband with despair, proved to him that he must renounce the hope of obtaining an heir; but since the page was not to blame for this, he fulfilled the promise that he had made, bought him a regiment, and resigned himself to having the most virtuous wife in France. His repentance was not, however, of long duration; he died at the end of three months, after having confided to his friend, the Marquis d'Urban, the cause of his sorrows.

The Marquis d'Urban had a son of marriageable age; he thought that he could find nothing more suitable for him than a wife whose virtue had come triumphantly through such a trial: he let her time of mourning pass, and then presented the young Marquis d'Urban, who succeeded in making his attentions acceptable to the beautiful widow, and soon became her husband. More fortunate than his predecessor, the Marquis d'Urban had three heirs to oppose to his collaterals, when, some two years and a half later, the Chevalier de Bouillon arrived at the capital of the county of Venaissin.

The Chevalier de Bouillon was a typical rake of the period, handsome, young, and well-grown; the nephew of a cardinal who was influential at Rome, and proud of belonging to a house which had privileges of suzerainty. The chevalier, in his indiscreet fatuity, spared no woman; and his conduct had given some scandal in the circle of Madame de Maintenon, who was rising into power. One of his friends, having witnessed the displeasure exhibited towards him by Louis XIV, who was beginning to become devout, thought to do him a service by warning him that the king "gardait une dent" against him. [Translator's note.—"Garder une dent," that is, to keep up a grudge, means literally "to keep a tooth" against him.]

"Pardieu!" replied the chevalier, "I am indeed unlucky when the only tooth left to him remains to bite me."

This pun had been repeated, and had reached Louis XIV, so that the chevalier presently heard, directly enough this time, that the king desired him to travel for some years. He knew the danger of neglecting—such intimations, and since he thought the country after all preferable to the Bastille, he left Paris, and arrived at Avignon, surrounded by the halo of interest that naturally attends a handsome young persecuted nobleman.

The virtue of Madame d'Urban was as much cried up at Avignon as the ill-behaviour of the chevalier had been reprobated in Paris. A reputation equal to his own, but so opposite in kind, could not fail to be very offensive to him, therefore he determined immediately upon arriving to play one against the other.

Nothing was easier than the attempt. M. d'Urban, sure of his wife's virtue, allowed her entire liberty; the chevalier saw her wherever he chose to see her, and every time he saw her found means to express a growing passion. Whether because the hour had come for Madame d'Urban, or whether because she was dazzled by the splendour of the chevalier's belonging to a princely house, her virtue, hitherto so fierce, melted like snow in the May sunshine; and the chevalier, luckier than the poor page, took the husband's place without any attempt on Madame d'Urban's part to cry for help.

As all the chevalier desired was public triumph, he took care to make the whole town acquainted at once with his success; then, as some infidels of the neighbourhood still doubted, the chevalier ordered one of his servants to wait for him at the marquise's door with a lantern and a bell. At one in the morning, the chevalier came out, and the servant walked before him, ringing the bell. At this unaccustomed sound, a great number of townspeople, who had been quietly asleep, awoke, and, curious to see what was happening, opened their windows. They beheld the chevalier, walking gravely behind his servant, who continued to light his master's way and to ring along the course of the street that lay between Madame d'Urban's house and his own. As he had made no mystery to anyone of his love affair, nobody took the trouble even to ask him whence he came. However, as there might possibly be persons still unconvinced, he repeated this same jest, for his own satisfaction, three nights running; so that by the morning of the fourth day nobody had any doubts left.

As generally happens in such cases, M. d'Urban did not know a word of what was going on until the moment when his friends warned him that he was the talk of the town. Then he forbade his wife to see her lover again. The prohibition produced the usual results: on the morrow, as, soon as M. d'Urban had gone out, the marquise sent for the chevalier to inform him of the catastrophe in which they were both involved; but she found him far better prepared than herself for such blows, and he tried to prove to her, by reproaches for her imprudent conduct, that all this was her fault; so that at last the poor woman, convinced that it was she who had brought these woes upon them, burst into tears. Meanwhile, M. d'Urban, who, being jealous for the first time, was the more seriously so, having learned that the chevalier was with his wife, shut the doors, and posted himself in the ante-chamber with his servants, in order to seize him as he came out. But the chevalier, who had ceased to trouble himself about Madame d'Urban's tears, heard all the preparations, and, suspecting some ambush, opened the window, and, although it was one o'clock in the afternoon and the place was full of people, jumped out of the window into the street, and did not hurt himself at all, though the height was twenty feet, but walked quietly home at a moderate pace.

The same evening, the chevalier, intending to relate his new adventure in all its details, invited some of his friends to sup with him at the pastrycook Lecoq's. This man, who was a brother of the famous Lecoq of the rue Montorgueil, was the cleverest eating-house-keeper in Avignon; his own unusual corpulence commended his cookery, and, when he stood at the door, constituted an advertisement for his restaurant. The good man, knowing with what delicate appetites he had to deal, did his very best that evening, and that nothing might be wanting, waited upon his guests himself. They spent the night drinking, and towards morning the chevalier and his companions, being then drunk, espied their host standing respectfully at the door, his face wreathed in smiles. The chevalier called him nearer, poured him out a glass of wine and made him drink with them; then, as the poor wretch, confused at such an honour, was thanking him with many bows, he said:—

"Pardieu, you are too fat for Lecoq, and I must make you a capon."

This strange proposition was received as men would receive it who were drunk and accustomed by their position to impunity. The unfortunate pastry-cook was seized, bound down upon the table, and died under their treatment. The vice-legate being informed of the murder by one of the waiters, who had run in on hearing his master's shrieks, and had found him, covered with blood, in the hands of his butchers, was at first inclined to arrest the chevalier and bring him conspicuously to punishment. But he was restrained by his regard for the Cardinal de Bouillon, the chevalier's uncle, and contented himself with warning the culprit that unless he left the town instantly he would be put into the hands of the authorities. The chevalier, who was beginning to have had enough of Avignon, did not wait to be told twice, ordered the wheels of his chaise to be greased and horses to be brought. In the interval before they were ready the fancy took him to go and see Madame d'Urban again.

As the house of the marquise was the very last at which, after the manner of his leaving it the day before, the chevalier was expected at such an hour, he got in with the greatest ease, and, meeting a lady's-maid, who was in his interests, was taken to the room where the marquise was. She, who had not reckoned upon seeing the chevalier again, received him with all the raptures of which a woman in love is capable, especially when her love is a forbidden one. But the chevalier soon put an end to them by announcing that his visit was a visit of farewell, and by telling her the reason that obliged him to leave her. The marquise was like the woman who pitied the fatigue of the poor horses that tore Damien limb from limb; all her commiseration was for the chevalier, who on account of such a trifle was being forced to leave Avignon. At last the farewell had to be uttered, and as the chevalier, not knowing what to say at the fatal moment, complained that he had no memento of her, the marquise took down the frame that contained a portrait of herself corresponding with one of her husband, and tearing out the canvas, rolled, it up and gave it to the chevalier. The latter, so far from being touched by this token of love, laid it down, as he went away, upon a piece of furniture, where the marquise found it half an hour later. She imagined that his mind being so full of the original, he had forgotten the copy, and representing to herself the sorrow which the discovery of this forgetfulness would cause him, she sent for a servant, gave him the picture, and ordered him to take horse and ride after the chevalier's chaise. The man took a post-horse, and, making great speed, perceived the fugitive in the distance just as the latter had finished changing horses. He made violent signs and shouted loudly, in order to stop the postillion. But the postillion having told his fare that he saw a man coming on at full speed, the chevalier supposed himself to be pursued, and bade him go on as fast as possible. This order was so well obeyed that the unfortunate servant only came up with the chaise a league and a half farther on; having stopped the postillion, he got off his horse, and very respectfully presented to the chevalier the picture which he had been bidden to bring him. But the chevalier, having recovered from his first alarm, bade him go about his business, and take back the portrait—which was of no use to him—to the sender. The servant, however, like a faithful messenger, declared that his orders were positive, and that he should not dare go back to Madame d'Urban without fulfilling them. The chevalier, seeing that he could not conquer the man's determination, sent his postillion to a farrier, whose house lay on the road, for a hammer and four nails, and with his own hands nailed the portrait to the back of his chaise; then he stepped in again, bade the postillion whip up his horses, and drove away, leaving Madame d'Urban's messenger greatly astonished at the manner in which the chevalier had used his mistress's portrait.

At the next stage, the postillion, who was going back, asked for his money, and the chevalier answered that he had none. The postillion persisted; then the chevalier got out of his chaise, unfastened Madame d'Urban's portrait, and told him that he need only put it up for sale in Avignon and declare how it had come into his possession, in order to receive twenty times the price of his stage; the postillion, seeing that nothing else was to be got out of the chevalier, accepted the pledge, and, following his instructions precisely, exhibited it next morning at the door of a dealer in the town, together with an exact statement of the story. The picture was bought back the same day for twenty-five Louis.

As may be supposed, the adventure was much talked of throughout the town. Next day, Madame d'Urban disappeared, no one knew whither, at the very time when the relatives of the marquis were met together and had decided to ask the king for a 'lettre-de-cachet'. One of the gentlemen present was entrusted with the duty of taking the necessary steps; but whether because he was not active enough, or whether because he was in Madame d'Urban's interests, nothing further was heard in Avignon of any consequences ensuing from such steps. In the meantime, Madame d'Urban, who had gone to the house of an aunt, opened negotiations with her husband that were entirely successful, and a month after this adventure she returned triumphantly to the conjugal roof.

The Marquise De Ganges | 49

Two hundred pistoles, given by the Cardinal de Bouillon, pacified the family of the unfortunate pastry-cook, who at first had given notice of the affair to the police, but who soon afterwards withdrew their complaint, and gave out that they had taken action too hastily on the strength of a story told in joke, and that further inquiries showed their relative to have died of an apoplectic stroke.

Thanks—to this declaration, which exculpated the Chevalier de Bouillon in the eyes of the king, he was allowed, after travelling for two years in Italy and in Germany, to return undisturbed to France.

Thus ends, not the family of Ganges, but the commotion which the family made in the world. From time to time, indeed, the playwright or the novelist calls up the pale and bloodstained figure of the marquise to appear either on the stage or in a book; but the evocation almost always ceases at her, and many persons who have written about the mother do not even know what became of the children. Our intention has been to fill this gap; that is why we have tried to tell what our predecessors left out, and try offer to our readers what the stage—and often the actual world—offers; comedy after melodrama.